REAL

CIRCULARITY

Real Circularity

The Practices And Approaches To Turn Theory Into Reality

Ken Alston
X
Rachel Sheila Kan

TheSimple*idea*™

First Published 2023

TheSimpleidea™

Published by The Simple Idea Ltd. (www.TheSimpleIdea.com)

DISCLAIMER:

The information and content provided in this book are for general informational purposes only. This book has been produced on a best-efforts basis. The author and publisher have made every effort to ensure the accuracy of the information presented herein, but they do not guarantee or warrant the completeness, adequacy, or currency of the content. Readers should consult with appropriate professionals or experts in specific areas if they require personalized advice or assistance. Explicitly this book does not constitute professional advice. You are recommended to consult with your local medical, mental health, accounting, legal and other relevant regulatory approved professionals as relevant to your circumstances and legal jurisdiction.

The author and publisher shall have no liability for any loss, injury, or damages arising from the use or reliance on the information contained in this book. They disclaim all responsibility for any errors or omissions in the content. Additionally, the author and publisher do not assume any responsibility or liability for third-party content linked to or referenced in this book.

Any resemblance to actual persons, living or dead, or events is purely coincidental.

By reading this book, you acknowledge and agree to the terms of this disclaimer. If you do not agree with these terms, you should not read or use this book.

Contents

"You do not belong to you. You belong to the universe. The significance of you will remain forever obscure to you, but you may assume you are fulfilling your significance if you apply yourself to converting all your experience to the highest advantage to others.

Make the world work, for 100% of humanity, in the shortest possible time, through spontaneous cooperation, without ecological offence or the disadvantage of anyone."

– Richard Buckminster Fuller

For Hendrix, Orion and all the children of tomorrow who will enjoy the Cathedrals we build today.

For Ken, sustaining life on Earth is a personal mission, safeguarding the future for Helen, Lyndsey, Harriett, and future generations.

This book is dedicated to our optimal collaborative collective future. A future where Cathedral Thinking is at the forefront, a future where we work now as a collective intelligence and consciousness for the future of all humanity. This context is bigger than who Ken & Rachel are being, it is about us all. We share this book in the spirit of this future, a future that is about creativity, curiosity and of course **Real Circularity™**.

Imagine a world where the value in products, businesses and systems are optimised, and accessed throughout the world. In each location we have fully operational systems and new locality economies that support the flow of money, seek to work with the intrinsic value in goods, collective intelligence and ethical application of these innovations for the good of each other and those living in its aftermath.

We want to speak to the people that want to create that world, it cannot be done with 2 people, 10 people or even 100. We feel that the reality of this collective collaborative future is dependent at the heart of the matter upon real application.

If we are to create sustainable circularity - **Real Circularity™** - we need for you to grab your "coffee" and join us in this exploration, as we get real, working on your ideas alongside our writing here in this book. Draw wild pictures, innovate, create new systems, start to think differently in your life, community and business or professional vocation.

This book is dedicated to you and those that come after you for all time.

As you read on, we give you permission and invite you to create from a blank canvas without ego and without judgement.

So grab your "coffee" now and join us in this dive into Real Circularity™.

Praise & Endorsements

"Preserving the world is often focussed on how we make things, but probably more urgent is a re-configuration of how investment is perceived and what qualifies as being rich. Rachel and Ken explore the relationship between such ideas with great insight."

– Dr John Parkinson,
Circular Wool Professional

"I love this primer on real circularity from Rachel and Ken. In addition to insights into what is real circularity and what is not, new approaches practices and examples, the book encourages, indeed inspires, the reader to find time and space to reflect and question circularity from an interconnected systems perspective. This is core to regenerative thinking and at the heart of Rachel and Ken's brilliant work at Real Circularity. One of the most important questions posed here, particularly in line of current nature-positive overtures is "How close can I come right now to align my business to Nature's sustainably circular principles?" Provocatively the book boldly and rightly makes the comment that most recycling is regressive, simply a down cycle to more waste, underscoring the transient nature of our consumption patterns. We are temporary users, there have been users in the past and will be in the future Something that those who seek a better, regenerative world based on more good need to reflect on both in lifestyles and business endeavours."

– Martin Brown FRSA,
Regenerative Provocateur

"I am honoured to work alongside you Rachel Sheila Kan. The old adage that 2 heads are better than 1, and 1+1 = 3 are reaffirmed every time we work together. A more engaged, collaborative and positive person I could not imagine!"

– Ken Alston,
The Trusted Authority on Sustainable Circularity

"Ken is an absolute hidden legend and it is such an honour to create Real Circularity with you, as a collaborator iterating the future together. It is honestly so creative, enlightening and I feel like we are jedi training together"

– Rachel Sheila Kan,
Ecosystem Architect™ and Circular Fashion Professional

Acknowledgments

Laura Storm, Giles Hutchins, Jenny Andersson, Daniel Christian Wahl and the regenerative practitioners in living systems design before them, especially the work of Donnella Meadows.

William McDonough, Dr. Michael Braungart, Walter Stahel, and many others for their pioneering thought leadership on what we now call the circular economy.

Buckminster Fuller who foretold much of what we now work on in Real Circularity. He remains a great inspiration to our work weekly.

Simon Hedley, our silent business partner who has worked with us to architect our work into a more commercial shell. His work in business acumen, branding/positioning and ontological aspects of being an entrepreneur have helped our work become seen in this world.

Aya who helped us to run and work on our original Real Circularity Forums where we were able to shape our work for the consultancy.

DaJeong who has helped us with launching and marketing our Academy.

Ken Alston, *Circularity Strategist™*

Ken is recognized as the trusted authority on sustainable business growth. His business career has spanned over four decades, including twenty years working in a global multinational fast-moving consumer goods company where he pioneered the development of corporate sustainability goals, actions and reporting from the earliest days of corporate sustainability.

Active in President Clinton's Council on Sustainable Development and the World Business Council on Sustainable development, he was an early contributor to business sustainability thought and actions. As Director of Sustainable Product Innovation, Worldwide, he was one of the first people to include the word 'sustainable' in his executive business title.

Ken changed from being an intrapreneur in a major corporation to becoming a consultant working with thought leaders and co-authors of the seminal book, *Cradle to Cradle - Remaking the Way We Make Things,* William McDonough and Dr. Michael Braunagart.

As a senior consultant, chief of staff to William and later as CEO of their Consulting firm McDonough Braungart Design Chemistry, he worked with dozens of leading companies on 'cradle to cradle design' and managed the startup of two influential NGOs. Namely, the Green Blue Institute, its flagship program, the Sustainable Packaging Coalition, and the Cradle to Cradle Products Innovation Institute and its product certification program for William and Michael.

Ken now works independently and collaboratively on the implementation of sustainable business growth with companies globally. He speaks at conferences, trade associations, universities, and in leading companies on sustainable business growth.

Ken's multi-dimensional fractal model - *The Ultimate Sustainable Business Cycle* - provides a unique methodology to go from 'meta' through 'macro', and 'meso' to 'micro'. Zooming in and out to understand the connections and flows between sustainability and the business cycle, based on nature's sustainable cycles.

Learn more at **www.TheKenAlston.com**

Rachel Sheila Kan,
Ecosystem Architect™

She is the award winning founder of The Ecosystem Incubator, Circular Earth & Real Circularity. She is passionate about applying Circularity and collaboration to transform the fashion industry. She is an author and is a sought after lecturer, speaker and consultant in the areas of sustainability, technology and living systems.

Rachel has worked in the fashion space as a designer and project manager for over two decades, where she saw first hand - as many do in the industry - the amount of linear product not only created by the companies that employed her but the immensity of the waste inside one of the most polluting industries in the world.

She started to work more hands on with sustainability and circularity, over time, helping brands to start up strong as well as create parallel brands. She has lectured on Sustainability and Ethics in business at a Masters level. Finding the gap between theory and application, she went on to found "Circular Earth", and in turn "Real Circularity" a consultancy specialising in applying Circularity to fashion businesses.

During lockdown, she founded a collaborative called "The Ecosystem Incubator" a project based on living systems thinking and regenerative design of business which received a Drapers Record award in its first year.

Rachel is living proof that tenacity is the way forward, she learnt a lot on the ground, meeting others, going to inter industry events and learning from many different sources Ken included, reading the tonnes of books needed to develop knowledge and then working to apply it in reality. Some say that she has a PhD level understanding of the subject.

She works with a pragmatic applied approach that takes into account the current systems and economy whilst bridging to the next one, at the same time utilising old skills and knowledge in the process. Rachel stands in all circumstances to cut through the BS and get to the roots in every aspect.

Learn more about Rachel at **www.RSKan.com**

Learn more about Circular Earth at **www.Circular-Earth.co.uk**

Learn more about The Ecosystem Incubator at **www.TheEcosystemIncubator.com**

Introduction

People have been talking about the concepts of sustainability and sustainable development for over 36 years.

The United Nations report of 1987, "Our Common Future" created the longstanding definition of *'sustainable development'*. Subsequently, the U.N. developed a global program with 17 complex sustainable development goal areas (SDGs).

Governments, especially in Europe, are increasingly seeking to regulate and legislate on matters relating to '*sustainability*' and what we now call '*the circular economy*'. More and more customers (and employees) want to be part of a more sustainable world and some businesses claim they are changing their products and processes to meet that demand.

Despite all of this stated interest in making sure we can sustain life on Earth into the future, we still find ourselves facing an increasingly unsustainable future.

The harmful effects of climate change and global warming are still on the increase. As we write this, higher and higher daily temperature records are being set across the world. There remains a significant persistence of poverty in the world; inequity in living standards, pay and benefits, especially between the developed and developing nations, as well as between Northern and Southern countries.

Food, products, energy, and materials are used and wasted in huge amounts and the systems we've created that run the global economy seem incapable of turning around to actualize significant improvements in local, regional, and global sustainability we need to see.

Materials are selected for use with little or no thought for their suitability for safe cycling as technical or biological nutrients after their use. Promised commitments by governments go unmet after major environmental conferences like COP, and businesses have, at best, a spotty track record on delivering REAL changes for the better.

So what can we do?

No amount of scaremongering on the apparent dangers seems to make a difference to policy makers and heads of major corporations. What progress there is, is masked or overtaken by setting continuous financial growth goals without sufficient concern for broader environmental and social improvements that need to go hand-in-hand with economics.

This book sets out for thoughtful, concerned individuals everywhere a new way of thinking, being, acting and doing.

It points the way forward for systematically encouraging changes in our individual and collective behaviours based on an updated reframing and restating of the old sustainability concepts that have not served us well enough.

This is an optimistic book. A book for entrepreneurs, for small and medium sized businesses with the ability to change faster than the slow juggernauts of existing big business. Or to give those juggernauts a new practise and structure to try on that would look at their work in a more lean and agile way.

In the past 100 years we see improvements in many measures of abundance, even with a fast rising global population. None-the-less, the consequential stresses and strains on the systems that create the conditions for life on Earth for all species are growing, not declining.

Real Circularity™ is a book for and about people who are tired of 'business as usual' and who want to play an active part in shaping the way the world lives and works for the better.

We will explore what sustainability and circularity concepts are, and are not.

We will showcase examples of people, places and organisations that are doing things differently, more sustainably, more like the way Nature automatically operates.

We aim to shed the old shackles of imprecise and inaccurate use of language that helps to maintain business as usual. We communicate clearly, and move towards honesty, transparency and greater precision in what we say and in what we actually do.

We always say let's stop 'talking' about it and let's get on with it.

Welcome to *REAL Circularity™*.

No hype, no BS, just practical, down-to-earth ways of seeing things in a new light, gaining new perspectives, combining together, collaboratively to co-create the outcomes we want to see for the benefit of life on Earth for all species.

Why Real Circularity™?

"Success is not final, failure is not fatal: It is the courage to continue that counts"

– Winston Churchill

There appear to be a lot of '*wannabees*'.

People who *want-to-be* associated with changing how we live and work locally, regionally and globally on this unique planet we call Earth, with a desire for making things better.

Look on the social media platform for professionals, *LinkedIn*, and search for 'sustainability' or 'circular economy'. You'll find a proliferation of people with one or both of these terms in their job title.

It is wonderful to see the uptake and interest in the circularity space, it seems that everyone wants to have a piece of it. The true irony is that we have to come together to create this in such unique radical collaboration, we must set aside our individualist ways. This is a difficult thing to be with when one has been in competition for such a long time, when it has seemingly been a fight.

Our unique 'trend radar' now sees Circularity in the centre bleeping away very happily - but really now we have established that this is what we need to do after 36 years of talking. How do we create 'Real Circularity™'? What does that look like?

It's a far cry from when Ken was one of the first professionals to add 'Sustainable' to his job title (as Director of Sustainable Product Innovation, Worldwide for a major multinational consumer products company), over 3 decades ago.

All the trends and interests are a good thing, or at least, it would be if they were all understanding, and comprehending the same thing when we communicate about complex concepts like sustainability and the circular economy.

In reality, there is a great deal of misunderstanding, miscommunication and misrepresentation going on. So much so that the real benefits that were intended when the United Nations wrote its now infamous 1987 report, *"Our Common Future"* has been lost.

We've reached a point where much of what you read and see online is what Ken calls *"Sustaina-babble"*.

It's the rote regurgitation of simplistic, 'received wisdom' from the past that actually turns out not to be so wise after all. It's the imprecise, unsubstantiated 'green-washing' claims from some who should know better. Talking as if you are doing something substantive while quietly carrying on business as usual in the linear economy.

Wherever you are on your journey in this we are here to bust the myths, set things straight and invite you to be consciously curious on how you can apply Real Circularity in your world.

You may simply be thinking about the things you buy as you live your life and also worry about the so-called unintended (negative) consequences associated with making, distributing, marketing, selling, delivering, using and ultimately throwing things away as you live your life - and you want to make better choices - personally and professionally.

You may be a business owner wondering just how you continue to create business and revenue in this world and move towards a sustainably circular business model.

You may be at work, seeing waste, inequity, harmful effects on nature, even sometimes a complete disregard for any outcomes other than single mindedly making more money. You like the work but feel bad about the continuing unsustainability of it all. It doesn't sit well with your personal values and you want to do something about changing the status quo.

You may be a student looking at your future career options with a strong sense of personal commitment to your own future and you recognize in your heart a need for more action and progress on these other aspects we include in 'sustainability' and 'circularity'.

You may want to learn more so you can be better prepared to help play a part in the changes necessary in the ways we make, sell, buy, use and dispose of things.

The question we hear all the time is, *"Ken/Rachel, so what can I do?"*

In this book, in our training, and our business consulting work we systematically chart a course that starts with your head and THINKING differently. Intentionally thinking positively about the benefits we can actively build into our systems.

- Informing you to help develop new understanding, new paradigms, new concepts, new attitudes about the world we live in.

- Influencing your future behaviours to more fully embrace and advance those groups, those companies who more fully reflect your sustainability and circularity values in their goods and service offerings.
- Directing the power of your purse or wallet and the power of your business budgets to activate entrepreneurs, movers and shakers who kickstart the move away from 'business as usual'.

Real Circularity includes and values economics, as it must, given how the world operates. It also values realising other benefits for humans and for other species too.

Real Circularity celebrates the improvements that many people have enjoyed in poverty reduction, food security, improved standards of health and sanitation, all set against the backdrop of an increasing world population.

The global economy has produced increased abundance by many measures, but we are still far from a place where the huge gaps in income, in health, in education, in food, in safety, in liberty, and security are narrowed to become much more inclusive of all.

Importantly, Real Circularity recognizes, and seeks to eliminate the many and varied **non-beneficial outcomes** that also happen when we live and work in the linear supply chain dominated, predominant business models of today.

Real Circularity looks at these "side-effects" and seeks to replace them with beneficial effects intentionally, by design.

Real Circularity is also sustainable. The action of closing loops in a circular economy isn't automatically sustainable.

There are many loop closing strategies that are circular but unsustainable. It's vitally important to be *sustainably circular.*

Real Circularity celebrates growth in the sense of regeneration. Do you really want your child to grow to be the height of a house or skyscraper, do we need a tree to grow right into space? Not really? There are natural regenerative ways to grow and encourage flow. New ways to make business that are about different strategies, future generational approaches that make sense both now and into generations to come.

The question then becomes, what do you want to grow?

For those of us practising Real Circularity, this means identifying and growing the top, and bottom lines on multiple dimensions (more than just monetary), emulating the natural cycle of living things, applied to both living and non-living goods and services. At the same time really checking in on what's so in your practise, brand or product as well as the bigger systems we live in.

At the end of the day we have to get real after many years working in the sustainability space, we can confirm that there is a lot of BS out there. Sometimes from a place of not knowing or delving deep enough or perhaps innocence, other times from a place of knowing yet doing it anyway and hoping to 'fake it till you make it'.

Our business partner Simon, always says that we must *"assume nothing and confirm everything"* this works in both business practise and drilling down to what's in everything that's in everything that's in everything. The BS out there in the market in every aspect even past the brand level and deep into the supply chain is a sickness of the system, the rigour is not kept or it is let go due to trying to survive in this world.

The main thing is that with these practices you can stop 'talking' about circularity and get on with some action in your respective business, consultancy or professional job. You don't need to be a business owner, much of what you can do can be intrapreneurial.

Equally of course this will be very beneficial for entrepreneurial players in the system. Even if you take this to your family level and employ these principles in your daily life, it will set a practice that will set you up for a more considered and curious approach to your life and work.

We ask you the question here, what is true wealth in this world? Sit and really think about it for a moment and we will be sure to endeavour to answer it to the best of our collective curiosity later in the book.

Observations:

Use this space to highlight ideas, insights and questions that arise from reading this chapter.

What is Circularity?

"The Pessimist complains about the wind: the optimist expects it to change; the realist adjusts the sails"

– William Arthur Ward

Circularity, or the Circular Economy to give it its full title, like sustainability, is a concept. An idea. It is a way of describing how materials and products in an economic system flow. In this case the cyclical economics of businesses. Until we create it in real life it is just that, a drawing on a piece of paper a 2 dimensional plan, how do we create this in real life? We adjust the sails.

The idea is rooted in Nature's sustainable processes, which are inherently cyclical.

In Nature there is no waste. In the end, everything cycles becoming valuable food (nutrition) for another system.

- A tree dies in a forest.
- The myriad of insects and fungi get to work decomposing and transforming the 'waste' of the dead tree safely into nutrients that are made available again, over time, as nutrients, via the medium of soil.
- All powered by energy from the Sun.

- All without contaminating life-affirming water and the wider environment or eco-systems.

It is worth highlighting that in Nature there is no monetary transfer from species to species for collaboration in sustaining life on Earth. The 'Economy' as we know it today in the monetary way does not exist in nature, indeed its first roots were not of money as Ken likes to point out below:

The Meaning of Economics

The original meaning of 'Economy' ('Economos) derives from the Greek roots "oikos" (meaning "household") and "nomos" (meaning "management" or "law"). An economist was the STEWARD, the household manager who was expected to practise good management, to be thrifty and live within our means.

The original sense of stewardship has been subverted in modern usage by primarily focusing on monetary aspects. This concept of stewardship originally extended beyond financial matters and encompassed the responsible and sustainable management of all aspects of a household's well-being.

In the contemporary world, economists are primarily perceived as experts in monetary and economic matters, often focusing on maximising economic growth, profitability, and efficiency. This narrow emphasis on financial aspects has led to the neglect of other crucial components of stewardship, such as environmental sustainability, social welfare, and ethical considerations.

The modern economy's relentless pursuit of monetary gains and economic growth has at times resulted in the exploitation and depletion of natural resources, environmental degradation, and social inequalities. In this context, the broader understanding of stewardship, which once encompassed the responsible care of all aspects of a household or community's well-being, has been overshadowed by a fixation on financial gains and short-term economic goals.

Today's focus on monetary aspects often overlooks the importance of simultaneously preserving and protecting the environment, fostering social equity, and considering the well-being of future generations.

To reclaim the essence of stewardship embodied in the original meaning of "Economist," there is a need to broaden the scope of economic thinking beyond monetary considerations and to prioritise multiple long term beneficial outcomes over short term monetary gain.

Maybe we need to re-invent what wealth really means to us as a business, professional or citizen. **We asked this in the first chapter so what is True Wealth to you?** We see it as the ability for humans to continue to thrive on this earth without depleting the ability of the Earth to sustain life, for its depletion will be our loss.

It is crucial to incorporate principles of sustainability, environmental responsibility, and social justice into economic decision-making and policies. By doing so, we can rediscover the true spirit of stewardship and work towards a more balanced and responsible approach to managing our resources and shaping the future of our global community.

In our human world of work, we've slowly become conscious that our economic (business) systems are linear and wasteful.

We take materials from the earth, make things from these materials (predominantly using non-renewable energy sources). Next we distribute, market, and sell these items. Finally these goods are purchased and used. At the end of their useful "life"[(1)] they are wasted. Typically buried or burned in a landfill or incinerator respectively.

> *(1) Note: our products are not really alive, but we imbue them with characteristics of life and often talk about product life cycles. Products and services should have 'use cycles'. We simply use most things we do not "consume" them. Move your mindset to USE not consume and you have a very different take on an item. I cannot eat these clothes or products, therefore I cannot be a consumer, I 'use' them therefore I am a user and there can be a next use.*

We have few cyclical systems in place to capture, reaggregate, reprocess and reutilize materials and products after use. The reverse logistics systems needed to complete the post-use cycle are missing in most cases. The future will be in these systems of take back so if you are reading this thinking of creating a 'circular' business or product then why not look at systems and processes as an outlet? The mining of products and their respective elements to balance out too much raw extraction will be a huge part of what is needed in the Real Circular economy, to support brands and their circular strategies.

Our so-called 'linear economy' is unsustainable and generates non-beneficial outcomes like climate change, pollution and many other unintended, non-beneficial consequences. Creating systems and functions that support take back, next use and looping will be paramount. At the same time they need to be sustainable, one can have a theoretically circular process yet it can still be at the very same time unsustainable.

Fundamentally, our unsustainability problems are the result of the underlying economic system we've developed over the past two hundred years or so. In order to better deal with the underlying cause of these unsustainable outcomes, the global business systems that are creating the "bad" or non-beneficial results need to change.

Real Circularity deals with an important aspect of business sustainability primarily relating to material stocks, maintaining their value, their management, and their flows whilst working with the systems that we have in place now, transitioning and bridging to future business systems. We didn't get to where we are now in one product design iteration. It will take multiple designs and redesigns in a continuous quality improvement process to get there.

It also deals with the question of ownership of goods and includes a time component connected to the definition of sustainability - sustaining the use of materials or products in their highest level of quality, and value, for the longest possible time.

By extending use, we amortise the embodied energy and extend material utilisation over the longest possible time period.

Our work in Real Circularity also helps you to flex your muscles in the capacity of working right down to a micro area of deep analysis then through the layers of the entire system right to world level, what we call a 'whole systems' perspective. Much of Rachel's work has been in the Regenerative space and this more holistic approach is more talked of here when we look at systems and processes, where there is over 40 years of research and development in these fields.

The old system in 'business as usual' often takes on 'sustainability' with a mechanistic and siloed or separated view of both the product, businesses (both inside a business in the teams and outside where business tends to compete rather than collaborate), industry and systems. Instead we invite you to become an eagle and zoom out to see how these systems interlink, how what you are creating in the micro aspect of what we call 'everything that is in everything that is in everything' links to those other layers. In short, to view this in a more holistic way.

The diagram here in Figure 1 showcases the whole system or nested system that we work and live in, you can see product or brand level is part of the whole and in turn it all impacts the overall health of ourselves and the world we operate in. Yet we focus on the micro aspects of the product more than how it fits into the whole system.

Figure 1: Whole systems / Nested systems

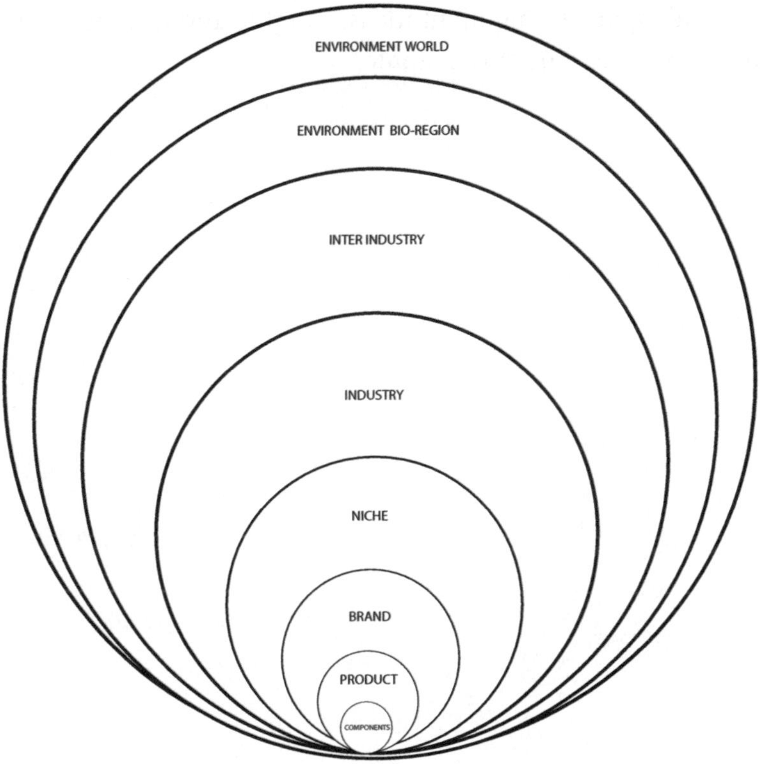

Observations:

Use this space to highlight ideas, insights and questions that arise from reading this chapter.

What isn't Circularity?

"When you focus on what you want,
everything else falls away"

– Brian Tracy

1. Circularity isn't "recycling on steroids"!

There is a common misperception that the circular economy is just about getting better at recycling. This isn't the case.

More recycling within the current linear business model does not change the underlying system that's generating unsustainable outcomes. It may improve the return and reuse of a few common materials like glass, metals, paper and a few plastic products but it misses many small products, single-use plastics, multi-material products and multi-laminate materials that are never collected in current industrial and home waste collection systems.

Plus, it leaves open the question of whether or not these items were ever designed to be safely cycled in the first place.

Much of recycling is also a 'degenerative' process, often downcycling to a lesser quality grade and eventually still moving into landfill or incineration. It is not the optimal end use for our materials and is not even optimally collected.

2. Circularity isn't assuming the materials you are using today are safe to cycle.

If you simply try to force and bend the existing linear business model into a circle, without understanding what the materials used in your product are, and how they interact with Nature, you are likely to create additional, non-beneficial, unintended consequences.

Circularity is based on SAFELY cycling materials in either a Biological system (like Nature), or in a Technical cycle for man-made materials not designed to cycle in Nature's cycle.

In BOTH cases, the choice of materials for the product or service must be screened and confirmed to be safe (from a human and ecological health standpoint) to be returned and reused. Remembering that the technical cycle is not a separate, independent cycle. It is still here on Earth IN the biological cycle of which we are a part.

3. Circularity isn't just making something POTENTIALLY safe and able to be collected, remade and reused. The cycle needs to be ACTUALIZED - REALLY cycled.

Companies following Real Circularity principles take responsibility for the goods and services they make, market and sell - even after the sale. They actively participate in the reverse logistics "take back" process either directly or indirectly. It is part of their intended design specification from the outset.

4. Circularity isn't linear!

Real circularity brings new, circular business models into play and changes the connectivity and communications you can have with your supply chain and customers.

- Are you sourcing materials, products and services that have been previously used by another company?
- Do you recover wastes and monetize them?
- Do you design and develop ways to make your products last longer, and be repaired?
- Do you share equipment or processes with other organisations?
- Do you offer the RESULTS your product delivers as a service rather than as a product?
- Do you look at the whole system & not just the parts?
- Do you talk to and connect with your clients/customers involving them in circularity at the end of use?

All of these have new circular potential to deliver reduced risks and more sustainable business growth when designed and applied strategically.

If you take the example of a simple cotton t-shirt for instance, you not only have to look at the growing process, is that Organic or Regenerative cotton?

You can start by asking which cycle (biological or technical) am I designing this to flow in?

Where is the water coming from? Is it possible to rain feed it? Where is its locality?

Is it indigenous seed? Is the place suitable for growing cotton? (do not assume that because it always has done that it will continue to).

You also have to account for the processing and one that is regularly not thought about is the dye process. In the actual application of the dye but right down to the nuances of each colour synthetic or natural.

Is the knit of the t-shirt mono fibre or mixed - does it mix cycles?

Then we have to work on the downstream, what then happens when it is washed, what micro fibres are released and which toxins natural or synthetic in terms of dye are wrapping the organic microfiber? Does the t-shirt wash well and give the user a certain longevity?

Then how do you get it back? How is it re-processed ? What energy is that using ? Where is that coming from?

How is it getting there and what energy and water is used and potentially affected throughout this entire process?

How do we do all this whilst making a margin for all the people involved in this seemingly simple t-shirt?

Back to the top is Cotton the best fit for this simple t-shirt?

Could there be other fibres that at each of these stages can be more beneficial?

What does beneficial mean? How does the T-shirt fit into other industries ("inter industry")?

Could it become a useful input for another industry? Could its waste chemicals or organic dyes be used for other things?

How does the t-shirt and its related outputs link to all the bio-regions that it is in from source to user?

How does it then in turn impact the world level?

Historically cotton isn't known for its social justice. How are workers treated and compensated today?

You see in one seemingly simple product that doesn't have many other major components how many questions we must ask and consider?

These are the basics and of course we cannot give a linear answer and stage for all things in one space, we cannot place a big brush mentality to this as each product, situation, business, industry and place is different.

CONTEXT is everything.

Observations:

Use this space to highlight ideas, insights and questions that arise from reading this chapter.

Why is Real Circularity™ so important?

"The best way to predict the future is to create it"

– Peter Drucker

The elephant in the room is the continuing unsustainability of global business and the additive effects of all the small decisions we all make individually as we live and work.

Much of the talk about what needs to change is focused understandably on "climate change" as this is one, (but only one) of the most important and pressing complex, unsustainable challenges we face.

Real Circularity is intentionally designed to move us towards becoming sustainable as well as circular. These are separate and distinct concepts and it is a critical point that many commentators and consultants never consider.

Bringing together these concepts is critical. Neither works effectively without the other.

Circularity is a means to an end. At its core, circularity is a key driver of change to the underlying business model that fuels our presently unsustainable local, regional, national and global markets. It is such an important part of the future that we live in given that the abundance of our materials and their value are now trapped in sub-optimal items that haven't been designed with circularity in mind.

Real Circularity engages with this principle and action of creating value from concept, through to creation, through use and on to next use. Value is designed to be retained throughout and beyond whilst thinking of the many ways we can tap into this critical value throughout as a brand, business, or alliances of businesses.

The end goal is to become more and more Sustainably Circular with each design iteration we bring to market.

Asking the questions:

- What am I trying to sustain?
- How close can I come right now to align my business to Nature's sustainably circular principles?
- What's in everything that's in everything that's in everything?
- Where does it come from and where does it go next?

These are just some ways to start this discussion and inquiry.

Real Circularity starts with increasing awareness of the problems and potential solutions. It brings new hope and resets expectations of what's possible. It increases dissatisfaction with the status quo (business as usual) and begins to set out new rules adding valuable knowledge.

Real Circularity moves increased awareness from just talk into action. From ideas to implementation. From understanding intellectually to practising behaviourally. To do something better, more sustainably circular than you did before.

For example, if you used lead based paint on my child's toy the first time, shame on you. But please don't collect it, recycle it and expose me to the lead again in a new product and claim it was somehow circular, therefore better. This is wrong from the start and wrong again when recycled.

This brings up another big point. Namely, the need to see the whole picture holistically as a system of systems.

Every business system is perfectly designed to get the results it gets - good, bad or unsustainable. Seeing the whole and the component parts together is needed.

In our Real Circularity work we zoom out to see the big meta system in which our unsustainable product or service exists. Next we zoom in to macro, meso, then micro scales looking holistically at the systems within systems, within systems that actually make up the way the world works.

We use tools and fractal frameworks that help to visualise how these nested systems interact. We look to Nature as our sustainable model and mentor, then bridge to our manufactured, (wo)man-made world to see where our designs are sub-standard and unsustainable.

Then we seek to redesign and reengineer systems to support the changes we seek. One design iteration after another.

Continuous quality improvement with every new or updated product launch.

Real Circularity recognizes that nature cooperates and competes simultaneously, so we emulate this by creating safe spaces for collaboration, even among people competing in a particular marketplace.

Two things can be true at the same time. Companies can choose to collaborate strategically on common problems like unsustainability and still compete in the market based on their creativity, design and other market criteria.

This *coopetition*, as it is sometimes called, represents collaboration between business competitors, in the expectation of mutually beneficial results.

Rachel's 'collaborative' The Ecosystem Incubator (www.TheEcosystemIncubator.com) is one such space. Together members of the incubator can join forces and, for example, can have more effective buying power together than each could create individually.

Ken helped to create a similar safe space for discussing sustainability in the packaging industry when he was instrumental in starting up the non-profit Green Blue Institute (www.greenblue.org) and its flagship project the Sustainable Packaging Coalition.

Real Circularity is so important as it systematically works on the how, the doing as well as the analysis simultaneously, the real practical application of circularity in this economy as we know it in a bridge to a future one. It is both generalist and specialist at the very same time. Ken's work with his proprietary fractal business cycle framework helps to break down the complexity of this action and system into bite sized, interconnected pieces.

Observations:

Use this space to highlight ideas, insights and questions that arise from reading this chapter.

What are the benefits of Real Circularity™?

"The greatest threat to our planet is the belief that someone else will change it"

– Robert Swan

Be Dynamic

Real Circularity is a pragmatic approach to Sustainably Circular business development. We know the pains of trying to apply things in a business setting and the kinds of meetings or strong conversations that you will have to go into, to 'sell' them to either your CEO, CFO or stakeholders, when being a part of a business or when creating or transforming your own.

Rachel was actively working in design and development in the fashion industry for two decades. Trend is a huge part of that industry jumping on the next thing and making money regardless of the outcomes environmentally or socially.

We can use that 'trend' aspect though as a catalyst of change to make a business case for change. Financial economics doesn't disappear in Real Circularity, rather it is a key mechanism we deploy to incentivise the transition to more sustainably circular designs by intentionally seeking better margins and optimised costs, even as we add in these new dimensions of sustainably circular intelligence.

Trend Aware

In our work we created the 'Trend Radar' to make sure that your business or practice is abreast with the latest trends and progressions .. showing what most people are open to or what nudges from governmental aspects would make your idea or iteration more commercial, less risky.

The trend radar, like in Air Traffic Control, is dynamic, shows you new and upcoming trends and presents them moving toward or away from the centre (where your business is) so that you can get ready for the next thing to re-imagine, or to prioritise the NEXT areas for attention. This increases your brand differentiation by being at the forefront of new ideas and not just those that are being seen now, but those that are coming up. Forewarned is forearmed.

We Invite you to be Proactive

As customer sentiment also moves into the middle of the trend radar we can imagine now sales managers coming into the design room having heard from customers and proclaiming or in many cases growling to a team "we need sustainability NOW" - and the design team having to scramble around to bring something semi viable together, this reactionary mode we always know is not an optimal space to be in.

We suggest being proactive and being ready. As a business, as a professional or entrepreneur, move with and get ahead of the trend making sure that you are comfortably placing this in your planning so when that sales person bursts in, you can say 'It's ok we have it handled'.

These trends can indeed be beneficial, a part of creating new revenue streams, innovative new products or parallel brands, iterations that look at streamlining, simplification, and reduction or working collaboratively to achieve the same goals. They can be a business case for change to take to your CEO or gather investment for.

Create new Revenue and Customers

We have often seen that contrary to the assumption that it costs too much, a lot of these changes can actually save the company money, time & development either in the short or long term, lending investment to the larger strategies and more complex structures which will need that extra investment.

Brands and businesses of the future will be held to account more and more, and it is important to be on top of that before it is too late. Ten years ago was the best time to start, now is the next best time, leave it too late and you will struggle to have a business that is viable for any future.

Be proactive and go after creating that future company before your competitors do or your customers move elsewhere, create future revenue and customers by being ready.

Streamline, work in Agile and Lean ways

Streamline your business to find 'acupuncture points' inside it, that can be short agile projects that show indeed, yes we can work towards a circular outcome here and make some revenue. Many call this 'low hanging fruit' and indeed it can seem trivial but often as Ken has proven many times, this can be both money saving and create change in that small area thus then having the next iteration revenue, validation, and proof to work on a larger problem and so on and so forth.

Agile iterations often then prove to stakeholders, clients or customers that indeed these new ideas work. If one is bold like Ken, you could as an 'intrapreneur' decide to showcase an iteration, he did this with packaging in one company back in the day.

They were very focused on using the same old packaging because that's 'what they knew'. He challenged that and actually implemented a micro agile project that proved that boxes from a 100% recycled source not only were more sustainable but they actually saved the company money. He strolled on into that project meeting to share the information and yes it was rogue but it paid off.

Now we are not all mavericks and Ken had the experience and management backing to know that it would pay off. We can at least set the business case for these small inner agile projects, more often than not businesses are open to trials to check more so than doing the whole thing.

In a micro brand environment you can test both the solution and the market quickly with a prototype or even digital creation or idea before you go for the full system. Iterations will make the proof of concept and will enable you to make good on the idea over a series of agile runs, ideas or processes.

Streamlining in collaboration with like minded businesses with the same interests can also be a way to create as a larger entity. This is a huge part of our work and we will be discussing collaboration systems and approaches later on.

Longevity in business and product

As an owner, executive, manager or employee in a company your objective is to create a business that reliably and repeatedly creates beneficial, sustainable outcomes. This includes creating 'longevity' in your business as well as your product if you have one. Indeed could the longevity be about making that product a service thus creating future recurring business with multiple clients, increasing the product longevity and the longevity of your business and client satisfaction?

The benefits of Real Circularity are measured by specific positive outcomes that advance our business and personal growth, sustainably into the future.

These are typically organised into financial sustainability, social sustainability, and environmental sustainability categories.

Different benefits accrue over different timescales into the future.

In focusing on these 'benefit areas' we can create for our business new and viable systems of change for Real Circularity that start to work with our business rather than against it. Bringing together new dynamics, trends, proactive growth, new customers, new interesting ways of working plus a future longevity. These can be used as business cases, personal strategies or within our local communities.

Observations:

Use this space to highlight ideas, insights and questions that arise from reading this chapter.

Old Approaches

> The problems of the world cannot possibly be solved by sceptics or cynics whose horizons are limited by obvious realities. We need (wo)men who can dream of things that never were."
>
> –John F.Kennedy

What Is Sustainability?

You were probably taught sustainability as expanding the focus of the business from its economic bottom line to include other 'bottom lines' in environmental and social or equity terms. Expressed differently, "People, Planet & Profits".

This is an okay place to start expanding your general knowledge and awareness. Simply expanding your business horizon by adding other related outcomes to your business scorecard and key performance indicators increases the likelihood that you will improve your overall 'sustainability'.

In reality, over 36 years of working on sustainability in this way has failed to deliver the promised sustainability. It's not that this way of visualising sustainability is wrong. It's just too simplistic, and not up to the task of actualizing the complex changes we all know we need.

These three "E's" or three "P's" are silos. Separate, siloed topics where the complexity of interrelationships between the parts is missing. We are often shown very neat diagrams that do not represent the Realness of the system itself, we acknowledge that in reality the economic E or Profit P is very much the dominant and must place that in to our work.

NEAT DIAGRAM ABOUT THE THREE PS

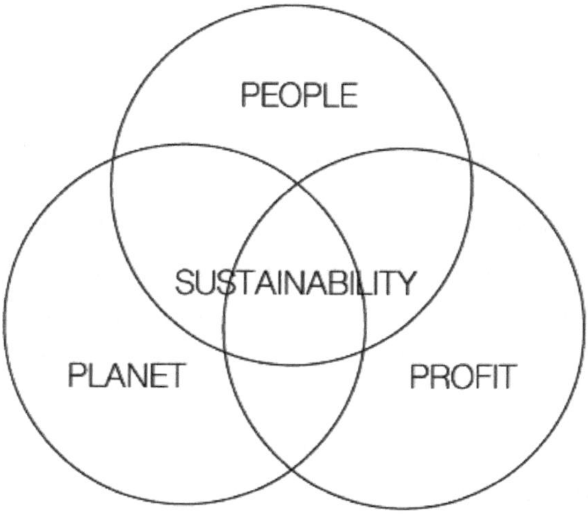

REAL
CIRCULARITY

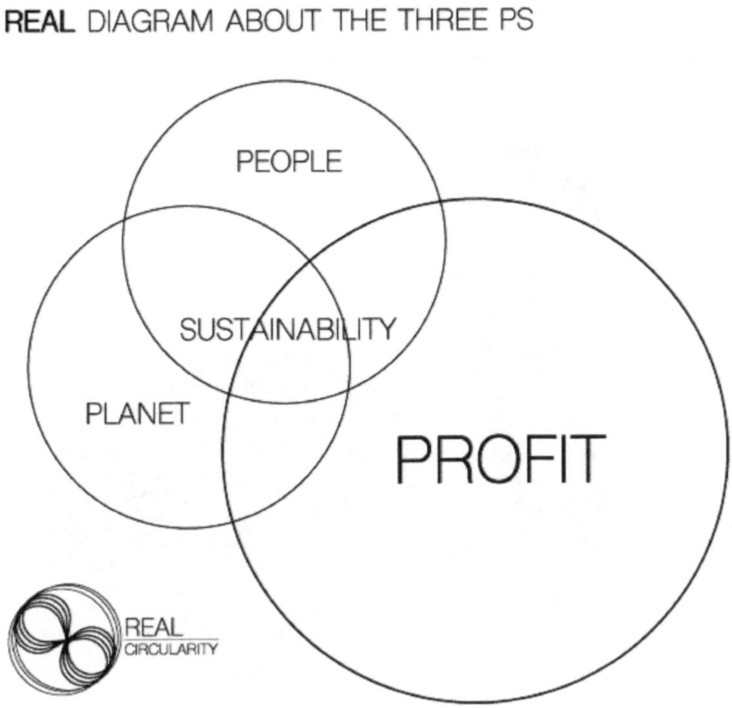

We Are More Than The Sum Of Our Parts

Our traditional scientific approach is often reductionist. We look inside the business, separate out the parts and try to understand them in isolation, then put them back together like a jig-saw puzzle.

Just as this diagram (below) of Vaucoanson's duck might appear at first glance to have all the requisite parts to function as a duck, it isn't a duck.

Our old mechanistic, reductionist processes miss the mark. We need a new, more holistic approach that better accounts for the underlying systems.

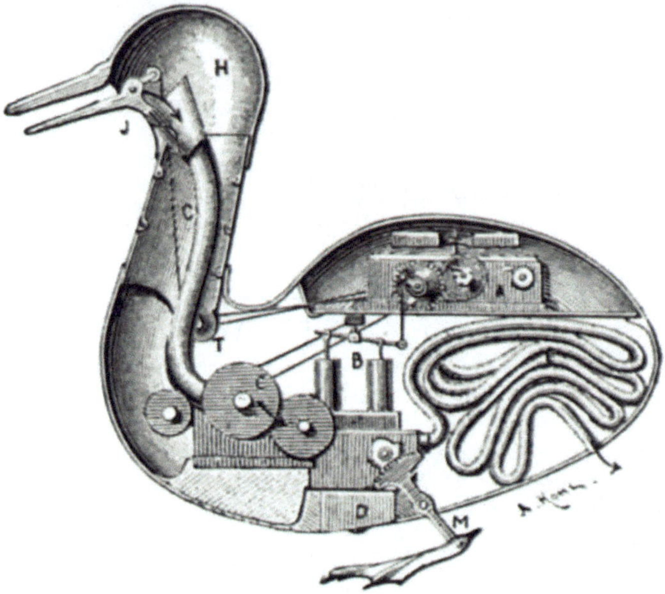

INTERIOR OF VAUCANSON'S AUTOMATIC DUCK.

4, clockwork; *B*, pump; *C*, mill for grinding grain; *F*, intestinal tube; *J*, bill; *H*, head; *M*, feet.

But What Is It?

- My packaging is PVC free!
- My cookware is PTFE and PFOA free!
- My t-shirt is PLASTIC free!

These are specific, clear and precise statements of what it's NOT.

But what did you replace the PVC, PTFE, PFOA and PLASTIC with? Something better or worse?

Maybe you used lead, uranium or asbestos! Who knows?

When we focus on what something is NOT, we completely miss the importance of what it IS.

Let's become FREE OF GREENWASHING by being honest, transparent, and factual in our statements of what it IS that we are making, marketing, selling, and using. More than just what it is NOT.

Efficiency Alone Is Insufficient

We can try all we may to reduce, avoid and minimise some attribute or outcome we don't want. But on its own this isn't enough to solve our unsustainability problems.

Back in the 1990's Ken helped the company he was working in at the time to reduce its virgin packaging use by 29% over ten years as a ratio to the amount of product that was sold.

A significant (and massively cost saving) achievement that helped win them the World Environment Council's Gold Medal for Environmental Excellence.

This approach of "doing more with less" is both ECOnomically and ECO-logically beneficial.

The so-called "eco-efficiency" approach is still dominant today because it provides a business with both a tangible economic gain and quantifyable progress on environmental dimensions.

It's an easy decision for any business to green light a project that makes or saves money and improves margins. But what is missing are the time based effects of continuous growth goals.

Assuming a 5% annual growth in sales, with no other changes, the savings in packaging materials from a 29% average weight reduction would be overtaken in about 7 years by the continued linear annual sales growth.

To be clear, eco-efficiency savings are good to find and important to do.

- They save money, so CFO's will "greenlight" these projects
- They also deliver a measure of sustainability progress that can be honestly reported.
- They slow down the non-beneficial outcomes of a business in motion.

What they don't do is change the underlying trajectory or systems inside and outside the business that are creating the ongoing non-beneficial outcomes we call unsustainable.

For this we need systemic change. What does that mean and look like ?

That is exactly what we create with businesses and indeed individuals in our work. Working with them on the whole systems perspective and setting a road map and a blueprint that makes sense and considers all elements of holistic design, business structuring and economics.

Many ask us about certifications, awarding bodies and government legislation. Legislations we feel are a great equaliser, and a nudge for businesses and entities to get started. Often they encourage the minimum or zero as a level which of course business will go towards. We ask you is zero or the minimum enough to really combat the real work that we have put off for 40 years?

We have people we have worked with that have seen fields of so called 'organic' cotton being sprayed with pesticides and so the great machine still continues on - we measure and regulate what is so, but also what isn't shown. The measures are not always taken with a whole systems or real perspective.

We feel we need a more holistic and whole systems approach here.

Real Circularity ™ not only considers the product, that's important but more so are the systems that it functions in not only in its production but in its user experience and back again. It encourages you to look past the current minimum standards and the legislation and get to the real heart of the matter like an investigative journalist yet have the foresight to be able to zoom out to its contextual picture and see how this information interacts with the business/ industry/ bioregion. Do not take what you see at first at face value, go and find out about everything and learn about its nuances so that you can call BS when you hear something that doesn't quite stick.

It considers and applies in a holistic way, not in a reductionist silo, in an abundant whole systems application. The below diagram gives some pillars to work from when you are working with a whole systems application.

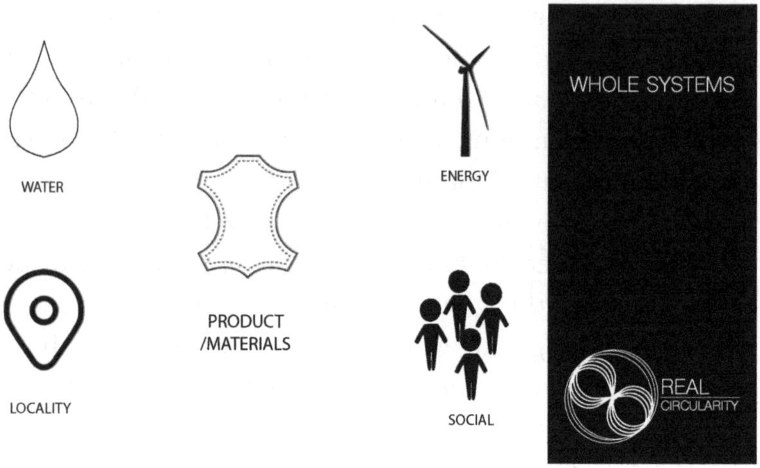
WATER
PRODUCT
/MATERIALS
ENERGY
WHOLE SYSTEMS
LOCALITY
SOCIAL
REAL
CIRCULARITY

Observations:

Use this space to highlight ideas, insights and questions that arise from reading this chapter.

New Approaches

"In every crisis, there is an opportunity. What if we use this moment to launch the world into a new era of sustainable prosperity?"

– Achim Steiner

Business used to be about stack-em high and sell out as much as possible. Then quickly find the next customer, rinse and repeat and hope that the next instalment of product would keep you going as a business.

What if we were to say that there are many ways to work a business. By diversifying your work and offers you might retain those loyal customers or invite new ones with your creative innovations whilst being fully circular or be on the way to being so.

The biggest challenge that your business faces today is how to stay in business economically speaking while simultaneously reinventing your business. How to progressively, yet quickly transition from unsustainable linear models to more sustainably circular business models.

Here are some of our recommendations, for you to start with.

Intentional Design

When you commit to incorporating these new sustainably circular requirements in your designs you signal your intention up and down the supply chain.

By communicating clearly that your PREFER more sustainably circular materials and processes, you set in train the change mindset from operating business as usual. You indicate in a non-threatening way that if a current supplier is oblivious to REAL CIRCULARITY that over time, they may eventually be replaced by a more sustainably circular alternative. Or preferably you work with them on iterating that over time as a team, often in fair trade brands and suppliers work more as a partnership and there is the opportunity to do this on a much wider scale.

You articulate an OPPORTUNITY to PARTNER on projects that are mutually beneficial to co-create more sustainably circular goods and services.

The two primary strategic paths forward are for existing or new products. With existing products, you have a more limited set of options because the key decisions on product design, specifications and business model have already been made. Here we are looking back at prior choices and evaluating the opportunity to make adjustments within the previously established specifications.

You might call this improving the status quo.

For new product development the scope for innovation is greater. Nothing is hard and fast. Except perhaps the perpetual need for a financially profitable outcome.

The design stage is where you have the most opportunity to change. Nothing is set in stone. The way is open to ideate new concepts, include new features, benefits, materials, business models, and communication.

Leadership, experimentation, innovation, the opportunity to apply new rules and create new standards is open for exploration.

The further you go into the product design and development process, the more choices are made, and over time, specifications get set. The opportunity to apply more sustainably circular elements gets increasingly constrained as product design and development moves towards traditional commercialization.

Choice of input materials

Can you source your input materials from previously used and cycled sources? Can your input materials come from someone else's waste or by-product output? If they are from a raw extraction, either natural or technical, can they be procured with regenerative intentions, designed for future cycles in more optimal ways?

Resource Recovery

Can you independently, or in concert with others take responsibility for the goods and services you provide such that at the end of use of the item there is a clearly designed, defined and operable path to recover, reaccumulate, and reutilize components and materials in another use?

Could you create a system rather than a brand? Systems of recovery are lacking, this can be regional or it could be hyper local. Could you create a new system that serves and maybe invites collaboration from the brand / business space.

Product Use Extension

Are your products designed for repair and upgrade with modular construction, ease of disassembly, and ready availability of components to facilitate maintaining the item in usable condition over an extended time period?

Can products be collected and resold as your existing customers upgrade to new models?

Precession

Thinking about all processes in your manufacture, shipping, selling, use by the user and after use .. where can you add in precessionary positive benefits of being a business and reduce the non beneficial precession (or unintended negative consequences).

In physics, precession is the effect of one body in motion on another body in motion at ninety degrees to the direction of motion. Our tides on Earth result from the precessionary effects of the Earth's and Moon's rotation.

When we are in motion living our lives as individuals, at work or in business we are in motion. As we conduct our daily lives and work there are side effects, consequences of our motion, our choices, that spin off at 90 degrees to our paths.

A little like a bee that goes about its business gathering nectar, in its going about its daily habit it creates a 'precessionary beneficial benefit', or side effect which is pollination. We as businesses and individuals can aim to increase the benefits just in being in the world, just like the bee.

We showcase and apply this with businesses and professionals by sharing our precessionary loop diagram and aiding in creative new strategies and application.

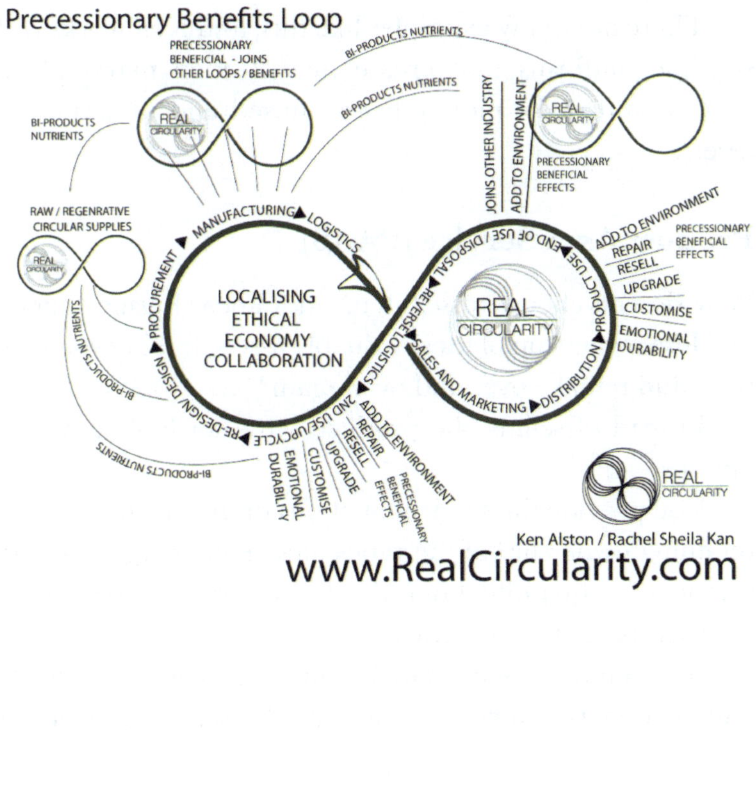

Sharing

Are the assets you own utilised to their optimum level? Are there specialised equipment or processes that you can offer as a service to others when you are not using the equipment?

Not everything needs to be duplicated and owned by every business. You can find new revenue sources by sharing assets that are underutilised.

A university Ken knows has over 1 million items of new and used furniture, and lab equipment in store. Not only did the university pay to buy (then not use) this equipment, they are now paying an additional ongoing monthly storage cost to simply house what they own but don't use.

There are many examples like this, and Ken works with sharing platforms that create new 2-sided marketplaces to save and make money from unused and underutilised assets.

Product As A Service (PAAS)

Why do you choose to sell items in a linear business model and lose ownership of these valuable assets, forcing you to go back and remake over and over again?

Instead of selling the product, why not look at service options?

You provide the service functions of the product(s) while retaining ownership of the molecules. You charge a fee per use or per a quantified output and commit to servicing the goods as part of the contract.

By retaining ownership in this way you can use the highest quality materials to ensure the service use time is maximised without the need for repair. You seek to make at least the same return as you did in the linear sales model - but you retain ownership of the asset, its constituent parts, and materials.

It is now in your financial interest to design for upgradeability and extended use cycles to retain your client and their regular service fees over the longest time period, while minimising the need for servicing and repair.

Communications

Your RELATIONSHIP and COMMUNICATION with the client changes. From 'consumer' to 'user'.

No longer advertising and marketing to try and retain the next linear sale, but rather engaging in establishing an ongoing connection, an opportunity to discern new needs and wants that you can embed seamlessly in your next service upgrade.

There is a big opportunity hidden here in changing the buyer-seller dynamic. Traditional advertising and PR agencies still don't get this. It's one of the reasons that greenwashing prevails. They just don't know any better.

It's why communications is a growing part of our service offerings in Real Circularity.

Streamlining

In the fashion industry many warehouses sit full to the brim with unsold stock, again costing money to fund its non-use. How can this be made more optimal? Can we apply a new thinking to inefficiency, how can we create better systems?

Collaboration & New systems

To reiterate the creation of the Real Circularity will need a radical collaboration of players and inter-industry models. Architecting optimal ecosystems both for business structures, take backs and creating new economics.

It needs new businesses to work on systems of take back and optimise the value of the items again and again. Repair systems and a value honoured in those skills.

It needs new systems of creating an economy that values the above in a new flow.

Entrepreneurs are popping up all the time, filling these gaps and experimenting with new approaches, unencumbered by the old systems of old businesses.

Speed

Ironically, the pace of change in business, the rapidity of new product introductions and brand relaunches - which are most often cited negatively as major contributors to over consumption - can also be leveraged as a force for good.

Make a commitment to continuous real circularity improvement with every new design iteration. Use the very pace of change to advantage by leveraging each launch with Real Circularity product and business design improvements.

By working in these new approach arenas and iterating our work and businesses to be aligned with these principles there is a possibility of creating real change, exciting business models and strategies that can be applied in so many places.

Observations:

Use this space to highlight ideas, insights and questions that arise from reading this chapter.

Real Interconnection

"There are no separate systems. The world is a continuum. Where to draw a boundary around a system depends on the purpose of the discussion."

– Donella Meadows

We - in our work - encourage everyone to think away from silos and to view what you are doing in your business, product and over all life as a part of the whole system.

All the while through this book we have been sharing a series of interconnections. In the systems and functions of the material world, the way that interconnects to water, energy, social and locality. The 'precessionary' creations of that material or business in its various states that it inhabits in the world. The interconnectedness of the materials and how they link into other industries, and how they interplay with the environment is paramount to follow as you work with creating product iterations and new business models.

How do these industries and businesses link together, and how do they interplay with government or wider world systems?

How does that work in connection with the environment, bioregion and overall the world? Do we now add the universe now as a part of our scope?

Realising how the nested systems indeed are a part of each other, can you see that what you create in one system will interconnect with another?

How will what you are creating have a knock on effect on people's jobs, mental health or happiness as a whole?

Often the social systems are not thought about enough and without thinking of this as a vital part of the whole system. Being paid enough for the job is one thing, being fully happy with what you are doing for that wage is another. As we speak the new 'trend' out there is sharing that people are looking for 'lazy girl jobs' Ones that pay well but you don't have to give your entire life to.

What if jobs themselves were just a thing of the past? Something for the industrial revolution and the 80s, where we look back and think wow that was really mad, just like we do cavemen or foragers, a land that time will forget.

As a regenerative business 'facilitator' Rachel does not want traditional "enslaved" employees. She wants to work with people who want to come together to co-create 'success' in a movement from ME to WE. Working with our life and energy, growing a legacy together and passing it on to the next generation.

It will take a new set of skills and a new style of leadership (which we are exploring and architecting inside the Real Circularity Academy™), to manage and master this movement from a mechanical 9-5 clocking in and clocking off model to a very much more holistic and productivity led model.

What is success in this world, why do we define it on one lever?

Many people ask if the business is successful, meaning do we make money from it? Why must that be the reality? When it comes down to it success can mean many things:

- It can mean helping many businesses
- It can mean giving a great speech
- It can mean making a great and important film that brings awareness
- It might be writing a wonderful book that gets shared
- It could be creating a beautiful song
- Or just being present with one's children and not having to ignore them to get some work done to be *'successful'*

Is our basic measure of success actually stunting creativity and ideas that would be successful for the world and its inhabitants by housing it in such a contrived box?

Real Success - or wealth - to us is the ability to live into the future not just for ourselves but for our future interconnected generations, thinking in generations is called **Cathedral Thinking**, we often cannot think about this time span let alone hold in our minds the multitude of interconnections for the product and business mentioned earlier at the same time as thinking about zooming ahead 50 or 100 years or more.

We often do not think about what we leave behind, what is our legacy to them? What do we leave them to clean up if we are not able to think compassionately towards the generations to come?

Like the great Gaudi who designed the blueprint for La Sagrada Familia in Barcelona, who created the designs knowing that it would take lifetimes to be realised. He created them anyway. Upon his death the work was carried on with his apprentice and still remains unfinished to this day. Teams still work on the complex designs and the future of the final realised Cathedral. The old sections sit comfortably next to the new and shiny parts, new builds onto old and so on and so forth. It's a true wonder to experience Cathedral Thinking in this way.

So there is an interconnection in things, in the many systems that we have, in ecology, in our ideologies, in social elements and in time.

Can you hold space in your mind for all that, in one go, on your own?

We all can try, however we've found that most can not. One would have to be a genius beyond compare. and then even if you could hold that in your mind like a modern day Buckminster Fuller, would you really be able to create traction without others both in the moment and in the future?

This is where we come to the word **Collaboration** or **Co-Creation**.

From Competition to Collaboration

Rachel has spoken about and created collaboration and co-creation in her business at its core. We have shared about it throughout and through our sessions in our Real Circularity Academy, and with clients we use its power to add to our business proposals, to work together on things and to collaborate with more people and have them collaborate without us.

It is a very alien subject to many, most get its concept yet we have very much been indoctrinated to the neoliberal past and present and its individualist ways. The free market was a space to create competition on many levels, both societal, business wise and throughout nations. Everyone is competing for a place at the table or for a chair and holds onto that chair even if it is uncomfortable for fear of loss.

What if we created business in a different way? What if there were chairs and tables for everyone? Maybe the chairs could be shared by 10 or 20 people at a time. There wouldn't be a fight then, only collaboration, communication and sharing.

Only after years of application are Rachel and Ken starting to see how this can actually be realised more optimally - investing the time to figure out how to structure collaborations and business percentages in this modern world and bridging to the future at the same time.

We are now seeing how we can all start to thrive - both in terms of money - but also through the value that we bring to each other with respective skills, different positioning and new opportunities to come together in different ways. Not just now but for the future us, the ones that will continue this work.

We encourage others to '*try this on*' and work on this inside The Ecosystem Incubator, starting with agile micro businesses from seed to store and back again - to come together and co-create regenerative practise in business. We are using the learnings from our work with the micro brands and players in this unique space to be able to learn how to apply the Ecosystemic systems practise inside our work with Real Circularity.

The main takeaway is that nothing in nature exists in isolation. Everything is interconnected. The only way to really thrive we believe is through Real Collaboration, creating win win wins with a Cathedral Thinking mindset.

Observations:

Use this space to highlight ideas, insights and questions that arise from reading this chapter.

Our Next Steps

Context is everything

Are you a business owner?

This is an exciting time and we can work with you in many ways to apply this work within the context of your business.

We all have to play our part. Real Circularity has to be applied business by business, location by location and team by team.

You can start to create and optimise your bespoke iterations, road maps and blueprints and prepare your business to thrive both now and for the future.

We host a regular forum online for exploration, sharing about Real Circularity and how it can be applied to business. You can register to join us live at the next forum or watch a replay.

If you're inspired to work with us or explore that possibility then the next step is to schedule a one to one virtual call. You'll find all the details about these options and more at www.RealCircularity.com

Education is Experiential

Are you a professional or student?

If you are an inner industry professional wanting to transition into working and applying Real Circularity, a student wanting to deepen your knowledge or a seed micro business wanting to start up strong. You can join Ken and Rachel in the Real Circularity Academy which runs over a 3-month period and is conducted through online interactive sessions.

Apply the workings to your ideas, in business situations and seed projects.

You can learn more about The Academy and apply to join the next cohort here:

https://Academy.RealCircularity.com

Speaking

Do you run events ?

To make your event 'Real', book Ken or Rachel as a keynote speaker. Ken is based in the US, Rachel in the UK/EU. Both respected speakers in their domains and contexts have been on large stages and used to showcasing their work respectively.

They are also able to speak at virtual events and masterminds.

Learn more about them at:

www.TheKenAlston.com and www.RSKan.com

Collaboration is key

Are you a micro fashion player?

If you are in the Fashion space and a micro business or professional look at our Ecosystem where we work actively on growing business together. Streamlining our autonomous businesses, co-creating brands, systems and processes.

We will be expanding to include other industries in time and already have a growing "ecosystem" of like-minded entrepreneurs.

www.TheEcosystemIncubator.com

Architect systems

Are you a systems thinker?

To Architect a collaborative as the ecosystem or an ecosystem inside a business link to our more macro business work. Link with Rachel Sheila Kan and Simon Hedley to create your journey as an Ecosystem Architect.

www.TheEcosystemArchitects.com

"Give me a lever long enough and a fulcrum on which to place it and I shall move the world"

– Archimedes

Leverage

The quotation above, attributed to Archimedes, can be applied here. You now have the fulcrum - Real Circularity - on which to apply your own lever.

Your lever is your business. Turn your business into a lever that moves the world towards becoming an economy that is increasingly sustainably circular by following the tenets we have discussed throughout this book.

Thanks for reading, it is now time for you to take action.

Practical Examples

What we have written about here isn't just theory. It's practise.

Practise that defines the leading edge of design and business.

Practise that embodies Real Circularity approaches.

Practise that moves relentlessly towards sustainably circular goods and services with each subsequent design iteration.

This book is intentionally designed to help expand your perspectives and hopefully change your view or attitudes on the possibilities for sustainable business growth.

And the next step - moving from changing attitudes to changing behaviours (both personal and business) is the main aim of this book.

As Bill McDonough says, *"Design is the first signal of human intention."*

The genesis of the Cradle to Cradle Certified® product and material certification program (Ref: www.c2ccertified.org) was a design brief given to architect William McDonough and chemist Dr. Michael Braungart by Designtex, a subsidiary of the Steelcase Corporation.

The original brief was to design a "collection" or "look" for a seating fabric. Knowing what they knew then about what we now call the circular economy and sustainability, William and Michael's response was to say they wanted to design what the fabric actually IS. Not merely how it looked.

Working with a Swiss textile Mill and the active, willing participation of the then CEO of the mill they evaluated almost 8,000 chemicals traditionally used in the textile industry and eventually made the design collection with just 38 chemicals exhibiting positive qualities that met their standard for safe cycling in the biological cycle[1].

(1) *Cradle To Cradle - Remaking the Way We Make Things, William McDonough and Michael Braungart, North Point Press 2002.*

Importantly they rejected the original suggestion to make a hybrid fabric from cotton and recycled PET. Such a 'monstrous hybrid' is incapable of being separated after use and cycled safely in the biological and technical cycles respectively.

In other words it had no next use designed into the material from the outset.

Their eventual choice of material was informed by potential users of the seating and their technical, performance requirement for the fabric to be 'breathable', to wick away moisture when seated, PLUS the ecological intelligence of a "Cradle-to-Cradle" or what we call "Real Circularity" type of design.

The resulting product, Climatex Lifecycle® became one of the most successful product launches with cost and social benefits to the mill, its employees and to the users of the product.

This first product to embody Bill and Michael's cradle to cradle design principles, began the consulting firm MBDC in the United States and advanced the work of Michael's EPEA in Germany. Later, as CEO of MBDC, Ken managed scientists in these firms to create the Cradle To Cradle Certified® products program and form the independent Cradle To Cradle Products Innovation Institute to oversee and run the program.

How can you start changing your personal and business behaviours? Moving wherever possible from unsustainably linear to more sustainably circular choices.

Case Study: Ken Alston.

Q. How does a company begin a journey toward business sustainability and circularity?

A. It can start simply with a CEO getting a sense that there's something appearing on the "business radar" that looks like it deserves more attention. That tingling feeling is your "spidey sense" giving you a message. You need to investigate this.

Possibly it's the growing risk that governments might be looking to add more requirements to regulations and legislation. Maybe the increasing number of calls, emails, or social media messages coming to the company from concerned customers about sustainability and circularity issues they care about, and need reassurance before they will buy from you again.

These issues may appear now to be in the distance and low-key but may actually be moving towards you at high speed.

I took a call one day from the CEO of a large office furniture company who believed his executive committee was not sufficiently up to speed on sustainability and what we now call the circular economy. He wanted a visionary speech to his execs to get them informed and engaged.

As we talked through the possibilities it became obvious that there was a much bigger opportunity to be had than just a one-off, 60-minute boardroom speech. Seeking to make the most of a major keynote speech by Bill McDonough, we settled on the idea to make this a bigger local event. Not only for the company executive committee but open to all employees and even the wider community, including their competitors.

By making this a big event with hundreds of seats available, there was substantial media coverage and PR benefit for the company, and a big win for employees and the local community to see the company paying attention to these increasingly important topics. By including competitors, they helped to grow their leadership position in the office furniture, architecture, and built environment industries.

But we didn't stop at the speech. As successful as this was in raising awareness, we added a follow-on workshop for the executive committee members the following morning.

At the workshop, I started out by asking what they recalled from the speech the evening before. In just a few minutes we had a long list of memorable one-liners from the speech that resonated and stayed in the minds of the execs. So, job #1, raising the awareness and understanding of the executive team was accomplished.

Once I had their attention, I projected their current website and the company's position on sustainability on the screen. Imagine their shock and surprise when they realised the size of the gap between what they were saying publicly, and what they now realised the business issues, threats, and opportunities really were.

What's more, a conversation with the person responsible for answering customer queries revealed a large and growing number of questions on the theme of how sustainable your office chairs and systems are (or not). The entire executive team was blissfully unaware of just how much CUSTOMER interest there was in the sustainability of their business and products.

Net, net, the CEO, and the executive team initiated a project to review their entire (extensive) product range and set a new intention to progressively redesign their products to improve their sustainable circularity with each new product launch or change. Their sustainability goals were updated, refreshed, and reported on.

This process of creating a new awareness of sustainability (and circular economy) opportunities and threats to business growth is as true today for most businesses as it was for the office furniture company several years ago. The risks of continuing business as usual are only increasing.

New companies are starting with the advantage of being able to design from scratch. Savvy companies are looking deeply at their business models and product offerings. Seeking to remain in business even as they transform their business.

The risk of ignorance and inaction on Real Circularity are likely to be more severe with each passing year.

This is the work that Rachel and Ken love to do.

Teaching, coaching, and creating new communities of practise that are literally reinventing how we live and work such that humans can do productive work, with fair economic remuneration and with design changes so that we get spinoff or processionary benefits (intended consequences) that help to support life rather than degrading our ability to SUSTAIN ourselves and all the other species here on planet Earth.

You can listen to Ken's Circularity Edge Podcasts here: www.circularityedge.podbean.com

Micro Fashion businesses: Rachel Sheila Kan

Rachel has been working with micro business and agile start ups for most of her life in sustainability. People with massive integrity, wanting to set up something purposeful that in turn gives them at the very least a modest livelihood.

A lot of her work ends up being business development, forming collaborations and partnerships. Recently she has been working with UK Hemp enthusiasts 'Contemporary Hempery'. Rachel is helping to structure the business to work with new ways of making money and collaborating to get the project seeded. Creating a fully re-localised fabric is at the heart of this business and decentralisation is a key part of the future and the stand that The Ecosystem Incubator makes.

Hemp growing stopped in the UK upon the dawn of the industrial revolution and the movement to grow cotton in India (we all know where those roots were made and who was degenerated in the process). In our unique Ecosystem they have found and started to work with other collaborators to solve pressing issues in the processing stages.

Watch this space as this is a project that is on-going. The Hemp itself is of course completely compostable depending on the dyestuffs that are added, the way that this is created will be paramount and we will be working with this as a showcase for regenerative practise and applied business in this field.

What's more, we created alternative business revenue by starting a Hemp Harvest Retreat to have enthusiasts in regenerative growing, fibre processing and new ways of working business come along and pay to be a part of the second Harvest. Therefore making a revenue stream that doesn't rely on a just product and is in turn educational, creating precessionary benefits.

This is the kind of business structuring and collaboration that has to go on at all ends of the conversation. Making business that has multiple revenue streams, that can create a flow between collaborators and create win-wins for the new types of business like localised regenerative fibre growing to become more viable. Structuring the possibilities of the future.

A lot of it is about past practise, a big influence in Rachel's work is a great man called John Parkinson of Iinouiio. He was doing 'circularity' before it was a thing, even before Cradle to Cradle as a child. She connected with John at the start of his 3rd resurrection as a business. John had been in what he called recycled wool or 'Shoddy' for much of his life, the art passed on from his father at the time we think he was one of the last people to know how to re-constitute the old used wool back to new fibers. This was actually a 200 year old underground industry we indeed found from his podcast. A somewhat clandestine practise called 'shoddy' where post user waste would be dropped off at the back of the factory by the dead of night so to be hidden from view (as it would have been seen as dirty to apply used clothing back into the system) However this is exactly what they did, to make it cheaper at that time.

The irony is at the dawn of circularity, John's Business was nearly at an end, it was his daughter who saw something about circularity and said to her father, that's what you do isn't it dad? Indeed, in a short 2 or 3 years he was starting again and found a textile partner to join with to make his new shiny circular regenerated wool a product again. A far cry from the word Shoddy. So circularity is not always new, it can be inspired from past workings that would have been lost or in the past deemed unviable- now new light can be shone on them. Take a look at what is possible and what is missing, you might find an old practise long forgotten, dust it off and hey you have the workings of a new iteration of old just like John's.

Here is a quote from John's forefather in the work of Shoddy that we found to be inspiring

> "Why bother to rake up the past? The answer is that there may be the explanation of the present and the guide to the future."
>
> – Rag Merchant (Herman Burrows), 1956
> A History of the Rag Trade.

Countless new business owners come along and want to get started in re-use, repair, upcycling. Rachel sits together with them and works on new business models that would create a flow of money for them and with them. How to brand position and promote what they are doing to show its true value and attract customers. Much of our repair system is informal and if it isn't it is too inaccessible or weird for a majority of people. We often say it needs to be made easy for a user to repair, they need to want to but also to have that want as quickly fulfilled as a new purchase.

One great new brand in this space is Rebel Patch, Lisa Matzi is showcasing an easy way to repair and to customise your gear by applying a patch. Not any old patch, it also at the same time showcases artwork from up and coming digital artists. This easy accessible way of working is a way to at least elongate some of our cherished pieces. Looking at the 2 cycles natural and synthetic we created one patch for each knowing that at least the patch could mirror a possibility for circularity over time, even if the items that it was repairing were not designed for that purpose.

The many Intimate Apparel brands and practitioners in The Ecosystem are also coming together in unique ways, where we work on streamlining their production and in turn manufacturing in their circular systems of take back over time. This is a mass or radical collaboration and will create a need for new products and systems that can then in turn be a business in themselves.

These fabulous examples are some of the great people inside The Ecosystem Incubator who have started to toil in a new direction. That's why collaboration is the glue that holds new economies together, whatever size your business or practise is, radical collaboration can be a part of your future.

You can listen to all our Ecosystem Podcasts and examples as well as our Regenerative season here:

https://theecosystemincubator.com/podcast/

Observations:

Use this space to highlight ideas, insights and questions that arise from reading this chapter.

Glossary

Sustainability: The ability to sustain something over a period of time.

Sustainable Business: a business that closely approaches Nature's sustainability, using clean renewable energy; maintaining clean water; choosing, and using materials as nutrients that are safe to cycle in either the biological or technical cycle. A business providing local ecosystem benefits; acting transparently, honestly, ethically, and with respect for people and other species. Overall, providing useful goods or services while simultaneously improving the conditions that support life on Earth for all species.

Circularity: The 'concept' of making and remaking things in a constant loop and keeping the quality, integrity of the item and value source over and over.

Cradle to Cradle: A precursor to the concept of 'Circular Economy' as described and popularised by William McDonough and Dr. Michael Braungart in their book, 'Cradle to Cradle- Remaking The Way We Make Things', North Point Press, 2002.

Regenerative: To create in the same way as nature's systems, either 'farming' regeneratively, regenerative business models where one mimics nature's cycles or as an individual in one's self development to learn to be with things as nature does. To flow as if one is a leaf on a stream.

Downcycle or Degenerative: A path of linear extraction and use that can only be on a degenerative path over time to lower quality and value. Refer also to recycle.

BAU: Business as usual, the ways of business that we have become accustomed to in the modern world. The extractive linear system.

Recycle: Is to make an item into something else, usually a downcycling process where the new product is a lesser quality than the original or a degenerative linear path.

Upcycle: The process of making something better than the original, 'I upcycle waste into a new item that has more perceived value than the original'.

Linear Path: The take, make, market, sell, use, and dispose (waste) general path of most items.

Planned Obsolescence: Where a company plans an early end of use to increase sales of more new replacement linear product.

Precession: The effect of a body in motion on another body in motion at ninety (90) degrees to the direction of motion. In the context of sustainable business circularity this can be thought of as the unintended consequences (beneficial or non-beneficial) that happen because the business is operating in a particular way. (for example - in nature a bee goes about its business gathering nectar - as a precessionary 'benefit' the bee creates pollination) Note that these precessionary effects can be beneficial or non beneficial which leads to unintended consequences.

Unintended consequences: the non beneficial, precessionary outcomes (from living or being in business) that are sometimes not intended or that often go unnoticed.

Inter Industry: Industries that are inter-related to the other industry. What can be the food for one industry could be the waste value created from another for instance. How does your business interact with other businesses not only in your industry but 'inter industry'.

Bibliography

Books that inspired us on our journey

Cradle to Cradle - William McDonough & Michael Braunghart

Designing Regenerative Cultures - Daniel Christian Wahl

Doughnut Economics - Kate Raworth

From What is to What if - Rob Hopkins

The Lean StartUp - Eric Reis

Thrive - Kees Klomp & Shinta Oosterwaal

Our Common Future - The World Commission on Environment and Development

Of Molecules and Men - Francis Crick

Operating Manual for Spaceship Earth - R.Buckminster Fuller

Regenerative Leadership - Laura Storm & Giles Hutchins

Reinventing Organisations - Frederick Laloux

Sacred Economics - Charles Eisenstein

Brands Mentioned

Contemporary Hempery - www.contemporaryhempery.com

Iinouiio - www.iinouiio.com

Rebel Patch - www.rebelpatch.com

Thank You

Thank you for taking the step to read **Real Circularity™.**

Please go to www.RealCircularity.com and look at our latest updates, and register to get updates.

Please feel free to share this book.

Do you know our next client?

We are committed to excellence in our work - yet keeping it real, and we are open to work with new consultancy clients.

The deposit to work with us starts from £5,000 and we invite anyone committed to REAL Circularity and a REAL business future to discuss their business with us.

In the first phase, we will work to gather results and look at low hanging fruit with a view to generate a positive ROI. From this point we then look to iterate the next stages with you.

This is a ideal fit for medium to larger scale businesses.

For micro business or professionals or seed idea, please take a look instead at the opportunities that our Incubator (www.TheEcosystemIncubator.com) and Circular Earth Coaching Mastermind (www.Circular-Earth.co.uk) or consider training with us in the Real Circularity Academy (Academy.RealCircularity.com)

Remember: This is Our Real Circularity Journey - we are not just about the product - we are just as much about how the business needs to run in order to look at the economic value that surrounds it, we get real, this is where we are - and this is how we get there.

We are ready to go - are you?

* 9 7 8 1 9 1 4 1 5 5 0 4 8 *
BV - #0011 - 020424 - C0 - 216/138/6 [8] - CB - 9781914155048 - Matt Lamination